FICUS BENJAMINA BONSAI CARE GUIDE

Everything You Need To Know About Planting And Raising Ficus Benjamina Bonsai Care Guide

ALEXANDER PATRICK

Table of Contents

CHAPTER ONE

INTRODUCTION

In case you haven't grown this plant before, you surely are unaware a way to take care of ficus benjamina. In fact, it isn't as tough as may also appear because ficus is unpretentious. Here are my simple recommendations a way to care ficus benjamina. Personally I think that it takes little time and brings lots pleasure.

As for watering, I endorse to do it moderately. It is also important to spray leaves with boiled warm water.

When human beings question me about fertilizing, I advocate doing it abundantly from May additionally to September once in 2-four weeks. Use organic and mineral fertilizers that can be sold in unique shops. Nourish the plant once a month from October to April.

In case you wonder in which to location the pot with ficus, I advocate retaining ficus benjamina exterior in summer time, as an instance inside the garden or at the balcony. But, avoid direct sunlight. In case you preserve ficus benjamina indoors, the temperature need to be at the least

$10°$ C and the air humidity – 50-75%.

CHAPTER TWO

SOME USEFUL TIPS ON HOW TO DEVELOPE FICUS BENJAMINA BONSAI

Leaves are the primary ornament of a ficus. Moreover, they are able to let you know about fitness situations of the plant. Observe simple hints to hold inexperienced, hard and robust leaves.

In case you see that young leaves are too little and vintage are yellow, it means that the plant lacks nourishing factors. You need to fertilize the soil or transplant your weeping fig.

In case of yellow spots look forestall watering for some time. This notion indicator about considerable watering.

Leaves may also grow to be dry and yellow due to direct sun rays. Shedding of decrease leaves is an herbal phenomenon, especially inside the indoor environment, but the barrel should not be completely naked.

Complete publicity of the trunk can occur because of delayed transplantation or transplantation in negative soil, unexpected changes in temperature and light regimes.

Brown spots on the rims may additionally signal about excessive temperature within the room, dry air or overfeeding.

Create slight situations to prevent ficus benjamina leaves curling, drying, yellowing and browning.

Foremost Ficus Benjamina sicknesses and Pests

Ficus benjamina diseases generally take place in leaves coloration adjustments. In case you cope with this part of the plant and water it fairly, you may not face such issues.

The maximum popular microorganisms that do damage to the plant are armored scale and carmine spider mite. The first one normally feeds on arms, lemon, ivy, asparagus, oleander, myrtle, ficus, and many others. Their larvae connect to the plant and feed on its juice. They're blanketed with a waxy defend and seem like a blade of grass. You can kill them with the assist of unique chemical answers that are sold in gardening shops. The course of remedy may additionally last up to a month. All the timber inflamed by using armored scales must be remoted from the healthy ones.

The second one blast is taken into consideration to be the most risky and tough to dispose of. Those creatures are hardly visible. I commonly use great ways to put off this insect:

1.   Cyclamen tubers decoction. Take 50 g of tubers and 500 ml of water. Boil till they seethe. Filter the liquid trough cheesecloth, and then brush the smeared trunk, branches and leaves infected with mites. You'll see that bugs disappear within 5-6 days.

2.   Persian chamomile decoction and green soap. Take those ingredients in the share 5:4

and 1 liter of water. Spray the plant with this liquid every day for 10 days. The enemy might be destroyed.

CHAPTER THREE

THINGS YOU NEED TO KNOW ABOUT PLANTING FICUS BENJAMINA BONSAI

Folks that don't recognize the way to plant a ficus benjamina often make critical errors which lead to the plant's dying. Planting a ficus don't need many efforts however call for following positive guidelines.

First of all, you ought to recognize that ficus grows speedy. The soil is to be nutritious because of this. A top of the line combination includes 2 elements of leaf and 1 a part of peat and humus. Plant ficus from March to August. In case you are aware white rind on the floor of the soil, don't worry. It is salt haze.

The second vital issue is transplanting as its miles and vital part of worrying for ficus benjamina. I'd now not transplant the tree in a bowl much large than its root machine. Consequently, carry out transplanting whilst the roots fill the entire pot. Humans frequently inquire from me while to transplant ficus benjamina. I continually say that the exceptional time for that is spring.

Ficus benjamina cultivation additionally consists of breeding. This plant propagates with the aid of reducing. A sprig should have an unmarried leaf with an intact eye and the lower 1/2 of the internode without buds. Cutting ficus benjamina you area several sprigs in warm water to the choice of latex. Then you definitely ought to split the edges of cuttings for higher rooting. Then cover little ones with a plastic bag. As you see, ficus benjamina propagation is alternatively simple.

Ficus Benjamina Seeds

You will by no means see a ficus benjamina flower and ficus benjamina seeds as this plant in no way blooms. It is bred with the assist of cuttings because it has been cited before. A few ficus may be bred with the assist of seeds; however it cannot be said approximately ficus benjamina.

CHAPTER FOUR

HOW TO GROW FICUS BENJAMINA BONSAI

You could develop all eastern sorts of ficus benjamina bonsai. Taking into consideration huge leaves of this plant you must plan the minimal top of ficus. I recommend you stop when the plant becomes as tall as 1/2 a meter. While young shoots are 10-20 cm, reduce them to five leaves every.

Branches maintain elasticity for a long time. This is why even vintage branches may be formed within the proper direction, using twine or without the help of a fitting device. For the reason that tree is growing swiftly in thickness, you need to continuously monitor the twine. It's far regularly had to trim the branches almost to the trunk to preserve a compact shape of bushes.

Ficus benjamina pruning for bonsai will take a lot time. in case you are prepared to do it often and are positive that you may not neglect about it, you may purchase a touch plant and begin turning it into a bonsai.

Ficus (weeping fig) has a shaky recognition as a bonsai: the species is vulnerable to losing the foliage and turning into leggy. But, in case you are determined to show a weeping fig into its dwarf sibling, test out a few styling techniques underneath.

There may be a extensive range of sophisticated strategies which help to create and keep the miniature length and form of a Bonsai tree. Pruning and wiring are the most crucial and well known.

1. Bonsai styling by way of pruning. If your intention is to create and maintain a miniature tree you will have to attend to occasional thorough styling and ordinary protection pruning. While you shape the weeping fig, you'll find out that one of the toughest things is to determine on which branches suit the layout and which of them need to be removed. It is endorsed to take the tree's primary form as given and try and avoid making any radical alternate. Determine what the front of the weeping fig ought to be. Taking this into attention it is going to be simpler to set up which

branches are to be pruned a good way to improve the general layout of a weeping fig. similarly on everyday pruning is important in making the weeping fig grow a dense foliage and broaden a branch structure, whereas the shape remains.

2. Bonsai training through wiring. In addition to pruning, wiring is a not unusual method of styling weeping fig bonsai timber. You will be able to set the form as well as attitude of the branches by wrapping copper-cord across the branches of your weeping fig. whilst doing this, start with the weeping fig predominant

branches. Bear in mind that thick branches require thick wiring. The cord of about 1/3 to 1/four the thickness of the department must be used. Try and cord two branches of one and the identical thickness with one piece of wire. It's far critical to hold a fringe of approximately forty five° whilst the twine is being wrapped around the branches. For that reason, you will offer a few space for growth.

3. Other Bonsai styling techniques. You could use lots of other Bonsai styling techniques to miniaturize your weeping fig. They include

planting rock formations, defoliation and developing deadwood.

Some other vital issue about slicing Ficus Benjamina

Even in case you aren't going to nurse a bonsai, you must trim your ficus benjamina as slicing has an amazing influence on the growth of the plant. I suggest you cut greater than 10 to 30% of the leafy bearing wooden in an unmarried growing season. My tips on the way to prune ficus benjamina will help you to do everything effectively.

THE END

www.ingramcontent.com/pod-product-compliance
Lightning Source LLC
Chambersburg PA
CBHW071644170726
48000CB00023B/1404